the Ordinary Seahorse

STORIES, POETRY AND PICTURES BY C. LAINE DOS SANTOS

FORM+THEORY
GUMDROP LIBRARY

Copyright 2024 by FORM AND THEORY STORE

All rights reserved. This book or any portion thereof may not be reproduced or used in any manner whatsoever without the express written permission of the publisher except for the use of brief quotations in a book review.

formandtheorystore.com

ISBN 978-1-0689448-3-3

For my husband, who has never seen me as ordinary.

I wrote this book to address unique stressors faced by children today.

Although joyful - it is not simple subject matter. It encourages kids to ask "why?", cultivate self-acceptance and develop empathy for other kids who may also be facing challenges. I hope it sparks many conversations!

You can go in order, read one topic at a time, or skip around and visit the pages that resonate most with your kids.

If every child could love themselves,
Find a safe space,
Feel heard,
And experience acceptance -
THEY'D BE FREE TO BE THEIR BEST SELF -
AND INSPIRED TO CHANGE THE WORLD SOMEDAY.

Here's to the next generation!

Claire Das Santos

Table of Contents

06 *The Ordinary Seahorse* — Paying it Forward	**24** *One Dragonfox* — Individuality	**42** *Beholder* — True Beauty
08 *Grit & Glitter* — Honouring Your Roots	**26** *So Rich* — Materialism	**44** *My Body is Mine* — Bodily Autonomy
10 *We All Have Rainy Days* — Sadness & Depression	**28** *Budgie Buddies* — Race & Diversity	**46** *Together We Shine* — Teamwork
12 *Love Grows a Garden* — Environmentalism	**30** *The Wolves Online* — Critical Thinking	**48** *Hamlet was Special* — Physical Abilities
14 *Pandachute* — 333 Rule for Anxiety	**32** *Pride* — Modern Family Structures	**50** *The Inside Donkey* — Phobias
16 *Light as a Feather* — Body Insecurity	**34** *Go Swimming in the Living Room* — Imagination & Creativity	**52** *Alone Not Lonely* — Introverts
18 *Warrior* — Girl Power & Equality	**36** *Down Deep* — Trusting Intuition	**54** *Tiger Bully* — Bullying
20 *London Duck* — Peer Pressure	**38** *Poopsie & Pontoofish* — Making Friends	**56** *Wonderful Thelma* — Neurodiversity Spectrum
22 *Glitter Buns* — Respecting Gender Identity	**40** *Ghost of the Seaside Deer* — Death & Grief	**58** *Lola Loved to Gossip* — Spreading Rumours
		60 *Secrets in this Book* — Take the Challenge!

THE ORDINARY SEAHORSE

One day a sea goddess was born - of seaweed and stardust falling from the night sky during a full moon. She was made of magic, excitement and all things spectacular. Upon seeing an ordinary seahorse she leaned in for a closer look.

"What an extraordinary creature!" she exclaimed

The ordinary seahorse just blinked.

"Look at your armour so gallant and strong, look at your nose so elegant and long! Your delicate fins are thrilling to see, I sense a whisper of royalty."

"Am I really that special? No one has said. You're Queen of the sea, so my ego is fed. I'm an ordinary thing, unimportant of course. Neither a fish… neither a horse."

"But you're filled with sparkle. I see you shine. Your beauty is deep and brighter than mine. So graceful and strange, to me you astound. I definitely need to get you a crown."

And with that, the ordinary seahorse was ordinary no more. She made him feel regal and unique. It was as if he were made of magic, excitement and all things spectacular...

Just then, he spotted an ordinary fish.

"What an extraordinary creature!" he exclaimed.

GRIT & GLITTER

They laughed then teased the unicorn,
When they learned where she was from,
They said her gold horn wasn't real,
That her street was dark and glum.

But she knew she was super fine,
A rare and precious gem.
A creature that could outshine most -
So she'd show all of them!

Her gold would never tarnish much,
From dirt left on the street.
Or from loving those with less-than,
Like the neighbours she would meet.

Her pride and joy wowed them all,
Her beauty and her brains,
Her glitter shone amongst the grit -
Like sunshine when it rains.

As sweet as cupcake frosting is,
Yet brave and wild and bold.
Eventually she galloped off,
But yearned for home I'm told.

And when she'd trot back into town
She'd show the ponies there -
That it doesn't matter where you're from,
When gold is what you wear.

WE ALL HAVE RAINY DAYS

Every single one of us... we all have rainy days.
Times when grey skies weigh on you,
In sad and lonely ways.

You ask yourself why me? Why now? Why must I feel so blue?
Alone inside your weary head...
Where it's dark and dreary too.

It's ok to share you're feeling down so others understand.
Some problems can feel oh-so-big,
And you need a helping hand.

It's fine to sulk and cry and pout, every now and then.
Just know that soon the rain will dry,
And the sun will shine again.

So snuggle up and take your time, sheltered from the storm.
A friend, your mom, your dad, your dog...
Will be there in good form.

Butterflies rest, and flowers grow, in times that aren't so fun -
So when it rains you'll simply learn,
To appreciate the sun.

Then rainbows come to visit you, in a warm and yellow haze -
It feels so good, you'll just forget,
We all have rainy days.

LOVE GROWS A GARDEN

Myrtle was a turtle, and he had a little stress,
The city life just wasn't his, he craved the wilderness.

So off he popped into the woods, albeit kinda slow,
Eventually he smelled the leaves and watched the river flow.

But he needed help from others, to keep nature bold and bright,
To love the grass, the trees, the sea, and never stop the fight.

He thought he'd plant a garden, to inspire us to care,
A travelling ecosystem, he could take just anywhere!

And when the people saw the flowers blooming on his back -
They'd all pitch in to love the earth, and keep the world on track!

So if you spot dear Myrtle, he'll kindly ask of you,
Recycle, plant a garden, and protect the wildlife too.

We need to hug the planet, and decide to treat it well,
It can't just be poor Myrtle - with the garden on his shell.

PANDACHUTE

Early one morning, An-An and his pandachute glided down to his new home at the lake. His anxiety seemed to grow the closer he got to landing. An-An's heart beat fast as he clenched his teeth with worry.

The panda bear moved from place to place a lot - this time it was all the way from the bamboo forest to the valley of the mountains. Which is quite a long way. It's scary to pack up your life and go somewhere new.

No one would understand his name, his language or what he would miss. Just then, he remembered his wise grandfather's advice: To ease your worries, think of the number three.

First, he named 3 things he could see - like the water, the snowy peaks of the mountains and his reflection. Now you try.

Next, he named 3 things he could hear - like the birds, the crickets and the wind beneath his pandachute. What 3 things do you hear?

And lastly, he moved 3 body parts - he chose to wiggle his toes, scrunch up his nose and flutter his eyelashes. Did you try? Doesn't that feel better?

And with that, An-An felt calm and self-assured. And when he landed all the lake-land creatures were so very glad to meet him. Welcome An-An, *you got this!* Three cheers for the new bear!

HIP HIP HOORAY!
HIP HIP HOORAY!
HIP HIP HOORAY!

LIGHT AS A FEATHER

"I feel heavy, and ugly." Ellie elephant whined
"I wish I was different, petite and refined."

You're an elephant Ellie! Keep it together.
"Why can't I be dainty and light as a feather?"

'Cause you're grand and majestic, powerful and tall!
"I'm grey and bulky, like a big brick wall."

Yet everyone loves you - especially your trunk.
"My nose is too big... I'm all in a funk."

But you've got the best ears and tusks oh so wide!
"They're also too big. I just want to hide."

We look up to you - in amazement and awe.
"But how could that be when I'm ugly and flawed?."

**If you just stand proud, and be only you,
Your gentle strength lets your beauty shine through.**

**Stomp on the ground and feel free to gloat.
Forget light as a feather, you're not supposed to float!**

**And why would an elephant want to be small?
Claim your space Ellie, you're the greatest of all.**

WARRIOR

The Warrior Princess was a force both gentle and fierce.

Battlefield butterflies shielded her from danger, while hummingbirds carried whispers of her enemies' strategies. She triumphed in every war, outwitting soldiers and Generals who didn't take her seriously.

After all... she was just a girl.

But her army was loyal, drawn to her pure heart, and nature itself seemed to align with her cause. She fought bravely to right wrongs and restore peace. For that, the people respected her.

And much like the velvet wings of butterflies and the speed of hummingbirds, she banished liars, thieves, instigators and bullies with a stern look and breath of fresh air.

She declared all people in the kingdom equal... even proclaiming the plants and animals were priceless and deserved respect.

She refused to accept the title of Queen, it forced her into a role reserved for women.

Instead, she would be KING.

LONDON DUCK

The London Duck was lonely,
And so, to make new friends -
He took a dare to walk the wall,
Out where the schoolyard ends.

He yearned to be included,
So scaled the bright red bricks -
And waddled right across the top,
To show them ducky tricks.

But what if whilst not looking,
His feet slipped, and he fell?
Would they try to catch him,
Since he couldn't fly so well?

They pressured him so badly,
Deep down, London knew -
He shouldn't need to take a dare,
To be part of their crew.

GLITTER BUNS

Who's that glittering over there?
Is it Joe, Joanne or Jess?
Is it Bob or Bill, Betty, Brook -
Or perhaps maybe Beth?

Is it he, she, them, they?
Whoever could it be?
Maybe it's just a Glitter Buns -
Who loves gold more than me.

Although to shine is not my thing,
It's cool and bright and bold.
I'm glad that Buns is glittering -
And living truth in gold.

Who knew a hare could look so good,
And though it's not my style...
There's freedom in the sparkling -
And that just makes me smile.

ONE DRAGONFOX

The Dragonfox landed in the sheltered side of the marsh, hidden amongst the reeds, cattails and bunny grass. Her delicate, paper-thin wings made the softest zzzzzz sound, then all was still. Her four little paws, black as midnight created soft ripples in the water as she touched down.

She was one of a kind. Like a secret. Like a wish.

No one else had her poofy red tail and black button nose. No one else could fly by the moon with long whiskers aflutter in the cool night breeze.

She was unique. Like a jewel. Like a seashell.

No one else had her big furry ears that could hear a pin drop, or a mouse sneeze a mile away. No one else knew that moss and minnows and daisies tasted exactly right together.

She was important. Like the sun. Like the sea.

No one else had her lovely brown eyes with flecks of gold and deep green, or her sweet little bark that meant she was ready to fly.

There was exactly ONE Dragonfox.

She was special. Like you. Like me.

SO RICH

Jabari the Rhinoceros, had always been so rich,
His parents gave him golden horns, such a dazzling switch!

They owned the whole savanna, fancy stuff galore,
Yet dripping in those riches, he always wanted more.

Then one day - POOF! - they lost it all, it started getting tough.
Would he still be popular, without his gold and stuff?

But as he rested in the wind, he heard the grasses grow.
He witnessed epic cloudscapes, and dramatic sunsets glow.

And right there in that moment, he felt it way down deep,
That money and his fancy horns he didn't need to keep.

For the world was full of riches, more astounding than his horns,
And they would make him richer than the day that he was born!

BUDGIE BUDDIES

The budgies came in so many different colours, from so many different places, and they all sounded different too.

Purple budgie came from where the wildflowers grow and sounded like a teapot.

Blue budgie flew in from the sea, his voice was like sneakers sliding on a gymnasium floor.

Green budgie was from the grasslands and sounded like the wind blown through a kazoo.

And **Yellow budgie** came from the blazing sun setting in the west and sounded like a squeaky wheel.

And even though their language was so very different, they still understood one another - they were the best budgie buddies!

They'd meet every afternoon on top of the zebra to sing, trade baseball cards and tell jokes. They learned everything about each other - and became better budgies for it.

(On a side note: the zebra was also fluent in budgie.)

THE WOLVES ONLINE

My older sister showed me a post that said a Carnival was in town!

Winter was just around the corner. Far too cold for a Carnival.

There was a ferris wheel, cotton candy and my absolute favourite, a carousel with horses that looked totally real.

Where the Carnival should be, was merely a lonesome, dark parking lot. Empty - save for several ravens perched on its broken street lamps.

But most exciting was Madam Mystic the fortune teller, dressed in a red velvet cloak decorated with sparkling jewels.

There was no magic. Only yellow eyes that could pierce through darkness… danger wrapped in velvet.

The post said if you visit her, you get a free toy that gives you magical powers! And you better hurry, they were "going fast!"

Urgency may lure you in… but there are no toys.

The fortune teller in the photo did look pretty magical.

It's not magic. It's social media. A place where things may sparkle and glow, but are rarely what they seem. Look closely my dear, beware of wolves.

PRIDE

All families are different - unique as can be.
They won't be the same, as for you or for me.

I know a house, with two dads running things,
Devoted and strong, just like seahorse kings.

Maybe your grandma is head of the home.
Like a tigress in charge, succeeding alone.

With unmarried parents, there's nothing you lack.
You're still a young pup within the wolf pack!

Stepdads buzz in, helping mom our queen bee,
He may not be blood, but he looks after me.

Sometimes best friends, can become family too,
They make up a herd just like elephants do.

Your flock may shift, as the years pass by,
Some birds may soar in, while others will fly.

Safe and secure, is what we all wish,
Moving together, just like schools of fish.

So listen young cubs, there's no need to hide.
Your family's majestic, you're one of the pride.

GO SWIMMING IN THE LIVING ROOM

Go swimming in the living room,
Go running in the sky.
It's all so easy in your mind,
Go on... give it a try.

Pet your glowing octopus,
Brush your tiger's hair.
Climb up great Mount Everest,
And meet the llamas there.

Imagination sets us free -
No matter how things get.
There's power in creativity,
When you swim and don't get wet!

You're the boss and you're in charge,
Of amazing tales and beasts,
Of fantastical discoveries -
Adventure, fun and feasts.

But when you finish ice cream cones,
For dinner on the moon,
Don't forget to come on home -
Have fun, we'll see you soon!

DOWN DEEP

It's ok to be scared, in the dark velvet night.
It's your mind's way of saying, that something's not right.

You know way down deep, if a moment feels wrong,
And trusting yourself, is a way to be strong.

It's called intuition, and it lives in your soul.
It's keeping you safe, and happy, and whole.

Poopsie & Pontoofish Had No Friends

The koala and the emu both felt invisible at times. Neither had friends, and neither felt secure or happy at school. Poopsie the Koala was used to hugging trees to feel better, it's how koalas are. But all of the trees in the playground had been cut down. So Poops just sat in a corner alone.

Pontoofish the emu had a "resting grumpy face". So no one ever really approached him and asked him to play. He wasn't grumpy - he actually had a great sense of humour. But his voice was quiet so no one ever heard his jokes.

They both felt alone even though they were surrounded by others... that was so un-cool. It hurt to be singled out and made fun of sometimes.

One day Pontoofish saw Poopsie crying in a corner. Poops looked up and sadly said, "I'm so awkward, I miss my trees." The emu whispered back, "You can cling to me."

Poopsie's eyes grew wide. He looked up at the emu and decided he really liked Pontoofish's funny haircut. He loved the emu's poofy feathers and beautiful shock of blue around his long fuzzy neck. So he jumped up and clung to Pontoofish as Koalas do. AHHHHHHHHH. Now that feels better.

When the koala hugged him, it felt really good. He loved Poopsie's leathery nose and fluffy ears. And for the first time he was confident enough to tell a joke. Poops laughed hysterically, and all the other kids turned to look. So Pontoofish told another, and another... until the whole playground was laughing hysterically.

It felt good to belong. To be heard and seen. And even better to have a new bestie for life.

GHOST OF THE SEASIDE DEER

My Grandmother died. I cried and screamed and laughed at the weirdest times. I couldn't imagine how life would be without her. Nan was my very best friend.

But one night in a dream, a magical deer appeared at the edge of the woods. She was so strange and beautiful, I gasped. Her soft eyes seemed familiar... gentle and wise, sparkling like stars just like Nan's did. She gazed at me kindly and said, "You are still healing from the day I left, but our love hasn't gone away. It's just changed shape. I'm still part of your story, always."

Pale pink ribbons floated in the breeze around her, reminding me of the dress Nan had worn the last time we played by the sea. I remembered the way she smelled when I hugged her close, burying my face in her neck. My love for her was deep as the ocean.

"I'll always be here, like a moonbeam shining through your forest," the deer whispered. "My love will guide you, lighting your path. When a cool breeze brushes your cheek, it's me giving you a kiss. When you smell fresh cookies baking, it means I'm wrapping you in a hug. And when you laugh, my soul will soar over the dunes and waves of your childhood."

I wanted to reach out and touch her, to ask her to stay forever. But her warm eyes twinkled as she said, "It's called grief, dear-heart. It's okay to have these big emotions. They might feel strange, but don't be scared. When you miss me, it means I mattered."

With that, the deer tiptoed back into the forest, disappearing through the waving ferns leaving tiny shimmering footprints in my head. That's when I knew she was gone... but her magic was still here. Her memory will stay with me until I myself am old and grey. She lives on in my heart, my creativity, my cleverness, my warmth and my family. So farewell Nan, it will never be goodbye.

BEHOLDER

Quick question:

Which is better - a Flamingo or a Peacock?
Both are birds.
Both have long necks and fancy, dazzling colours.
Both are extraordinarily beautiful.
But... which one is *better*?

The answer is BOTH.

Everyone sees beauty in different ways for different reasons. That's what "in the eye of the beholder" means.

Just like one bird isn't "better" than the other, one person isn't "better" either. Remember that no one is ever truly ugly on the outside - because someone somewhere will see them as beautiful.

How lovely is that!

MY BODY IS MINE

Polar bear wanted to snuggle rabbit.
Rabbit said: No thank you.

Then Polar Bear asked: Can I pet you Rabbit?
Rabbit said: DO NOT TOUCH ME PLEASE.

Next, Polar bear said: What about a nice big hug?
Rabbit said: My body is mine. It's not yours to touch. I protect my personal space, and *you* Polar Bear, make me feel uncomfortable.

Polar bear growled: I'm bigger than you. I'm older than you. You should do as I say.

But Rabbit had been taught about "unsafe touch", and knew saying NO was always allowed. This knowledge was Rabbit's armour.

Rabbit replied: Being small and young doesn't change anything, my body belongs to me. SO PAWS OFF.

And with that Rabbit hopped to a safe space to find a trusted adult and tell them all about Polar Bear. Knowledge keeps you safe, and speaking up is important. It wasn't easy, but Rabbit would keep telling, telling, telling and telling... until *this* little bunny was heard.

TOGETHER WE SHINE

12 little ferrets
up in the chandelier.
How in the heck
did we end up here?

One couldn't do it,
not even four or five,
but with a furry dozen,
our dream was realized!

We teamed up together,
a secret plan was hatched,
to get us to the ceiling,
we each had a task.

With much determination,
up and up we climbed.
Our squad became one.
'Cause together we shine.

now... how do we get down...

HAMLET WAS SPECIAL

Hamlet went and lost his eye,
While doing piggy things.
The doctors patched him up just right,
So now he laughs and sings!

He colours, runs, and plays all day,
In games of "Tag! You're it!"
His eye patch never slows him down,
He's strong, and fast, and fit.

Here and there a helping hand,
Will aide him on his way.
He's always learning neat new things,
To chase and seize the day!

Some piggies cannot walk or run,
And some can't hear or speak.
But they all have great abilities,
Like Hamlet, they're unique!

So when you see this piggy,
Doing little piggy things,
Join him for a game of tag -
And listen to him sing!

Hamlet's cool and different,
It's clear for all to see,
I hope he'll think I'm fun enough -
To be best friends with me!

THE INSIDE DONKEY

Once there was a donkey who felt nervous about the big wide world outside. "A phobia" they called it. He didn't know exactly what that meant, but it kept him stuck in his camper van, looking out longingly at the moody desert grassland stretching far and wide. He dreamed of exploring it as an adventurous wild beast, yet he only knew the squeaky camper van floor beneath his hooves instead of warm sand or cool grass.

Inside, he'd listen to the lights buzzing, never feeling the sunshine on his back or the gentle breeze combing through his fur. What a funny, yet sad life for a donkey, don't you think?

What if stepping beyond what scares us can reveal surprising treasures? What if the things you're missing out on, are even more amazing than you ever imagined?

It's not easy to face our fears. But think of our friend the donkey. Wouldn't you want him to feel the thrill of galloping through the desert, kicking up clouds of dust like a mighty stallion? To sniff a cactus flower as it blooms in the morning sun... then gobble it up for lunch? Or meeting other wild beastie donkeys who could "HEEEEE-HAAAAWWW" by his side?

Sometimes, we're all a bit like that inside donkey. We feel safe staying put. But don't stay indoors too long, little one.

In the wild is where you're free.

ALONE NOT LONELY

Sitting alone in my rickety wooden boat,
I'm happy by myself, I like to think and float.
While others need noise and lots of this and that,
I prefer it when it's calm.. and quiet.. and flat.

When someone tries to tell me alone is very sad,
I smile to myself, and cherish time I've had -
To sit alone in my rickety wooden boat
I'm alone not lonely - and that always gets my vote.

TIGER BULLY

A bully is like a tiger… on roller skates.

He tries to look fierce, flashing his fangs and flexing his claws, growling and roaring to keep everyone scared. But look closely - He doesn't have balance. Under all that bravado, he's shaky and unsure, afraid someone might see how insecure *he* actually feels.

The minute you challenge the tiger by standing up for yourself, or for supporting somebody else, or telling a grownup about his lousy tiger 'tude, well… his wheels start to wobble. The more of you that stand on solid ground together, the less balance the tiger will have.

I mean… how ridiculous is that tiger flailing about? He's not even wearing a helmet!

That beast needs to take a seat and chill out, it's your turn to roar.

WONDERFUL THELMA

This is Thelma. Beautiful, wonderful Thelma.

Thelma has a heart as big as the forest, but she worries about things that others don't even notice. Like before bed, she turns her nightlight on and off exactly ten times, just to be sure it'll shine bright through the night.

Thelma loves flowers, so she spends as much time as possible in the garden. She watches the fuzzy bumblebees intently, counting each one as they buzzzzz by delicate petals. Counting is her *very favourite thing*, but it makes it tricky to play with others... I mean it's pretty hard when you have to count all the time!

And she absolutely hates green beans - they remind her of worms. Oh dear.

She needs to move slow.
She likes things that aren't loud or busy.
And sometimes she gets confused when too many birds are singing.

But because she listens so carefully, Thelma knows every bird's song by heart. She even understands the secret stories ants whisper as they scurry by, little secrets that others miss because they're too busy talking. (She counts the ants too.)

Her slow pace means she spots things a chipmunk or cheetah might miss - like a baby mouse napping under a toadstool, sparkles in raindrops, or the softest shade of purple in a butterfly's wings.

So slow down a minute. Get to know Thelma. Because our differences make the world a better place. And Thelma's world... well, it's wonderful.

LOLA LOVED TO GOSSIP

Lola loved to gossip,
About monkeys in her school.
She'd make up little tidbits,
Just stuff that wasn't cool.

She'd whisper on the playground,
She'd talk over the phone,
She'd text her classroom besties,
Each time she was alone.

I tried to tell her it was mean,
But she just couldn't see.
And then she turned around
And made some gossip about me!

Then one day other monkeys
Started rumours about her,
She tried to stop the whispers,
When it got under her fur.

And so right then dear Lola,
Stopped her nasty gossip game.
As it wasn't very fair or nice,
For her to do the same.

Don't be a silly monkey,
Stop rumours right away.
And tell those out there gossiping,
It could be them someday.

SECRETS IN THIS BOOK.

Every morning when seahorses wake up and see their mate, they greet each other with a special secret dance, sometimes even changing colour!
Male seahorses take care of the babies, carrying them in their pouch just like kangaroos.

Only 1 in 100,000 female deer have antlers, making them magically rare.

Tortoises are part of the turtle family and have been around for more than 200 million years. Wow. That's a crazy long time. How old are you?

Flamingos and peacocks both have loud raunchy squawks! For such beautiful birds, their voices are pretty funny.

Did you know that foxes can climb trees? They're agile and muscular - and they have retractable claws that allow them to grip the bark. Whoosh! So fast!

Pandas live in China and eat 26 to 84 pounds of bamboo *a day*! That's a lot of food. But they're about as big as a small couch - so they get hungry.

Sloths are herbivores. They love to eat flowers as a special treat - like bright red Hibiscus or hot pink Bougainvillea.

Butterflies do indeed rest when it rains. To prevent getting wet, they hide under leaves and in the crevices of rocks. They can't fly with wet wings so they stay put until the storm passes.

TAKE THE "EXTRAORDINARY SEAHORSE" EVERYDAY CHALLENGE:
1. Share something every day - a thought, a toy or even dessert! 2. Pick up litter when you see it. 3. Smile at someone you know has few friends. 4. Read a little. 5. Try something completely new!
THANK YOU FOR BEING EXTRAORDINARY!

www.ingramcontent.com/pod-product-compliance
Lightning Source LLC
Chambersburg PA
CBHW060820090426
42738CB00002B/57